AF381329

MIGUEL DE CERVANTES

The father of Don Quixote

Written by Constantin Maes
In collaboration with Nathalie Hancisse
Translated by Rebecca Neal

Art & Literature 50MINUTES.com

MIGUEL DE CERVANTES

- **Name:** Miguel de Cervantes Saavedra.
- **Born:** around 29 September 1547 in Alcalá de Henares, near Madrid.
- **Died:** buried on 23 April 1616 in Madrid.
- **Context:** during Cervantes's time, Spain was undergoing a period of political decline, but this was offset by a flourishing cultural scene, with considerable developments across all the arts and particularly in literature.
- **Notable works:**
  - *The Siege of Numantia* (1585), play
  - *La Galatea* (1585), pastoral romance
  - *Don Quixote* (first volume 1605; second volume 1615), novel
  - *Novelas ejemplares* (1613), collection of novellas
  - *The Trials of Persiles and Sigismunda* (1617), novel

Miguel de Cervantes is a towering figure of 16th- and 17th-century Spanish literature, and is widely considered to be the country's greatest ever writer. In spite of his relatively humble origins, his life was almost as adventure-packed as those of his heroes, with stints as the secretary of a future cardinal, a soldier, a prisoner of war, a tax collector and a fugitive suspected of murder. Even so, he somehow found the time to produce a vast body of work, comprising poems, plays, novellas and novels, between 1569 and his death in 1616.

It is worth mentioning that Cervantes was working in a context that provided no shortage of inspiration: the Spanish Golden Age. Although the country was declining politically, its artistic output was thriving. Painters, writers, architects and musicians reached dizzying heights of creativity and produced some of Spain's greatest masterpieces. In spite of his undeniable talent for theatre and poetry, Cervantes could not match the innovations of his contemporaries in these fields; instead, he left his mark on literature with his novels and novellas. By parodying earlier forms, in particular the chivalric romance, he left his mark on the genre of the picaresque novel, an adventure story packed with outlandish situations and colourful characters. Even today, over 400 years after it was first published, the humour and absurdity of *Don Quixote*, which he first dreamed up when he was in prison, continue to captivate readers around the world.

| Between 1925 and 1930, a monument in me-

mory of Cervantes, created by the architects Rafael Martínez Zapatero and Pedro Muguruza, and the sculptor Lorenzo Coullaut Valera, was erected in Madrid's Plaza de España, a clear testament to his importance in Spanish literature. The monument comprises stone sculptures of Cervantes (in the centre) and Aldonza Lorenzo, better known as Dulcinea in *Don Quixote*, as well as two bronze sculptures of Don Quixote and his squire Sancho Panza.

CONTEXT

SPAIN'S GLOBAL EMPIRE DURING THE 16TH CENTURY

During the second half of the 16th century, Spain ruled over a vast territory which it had acquired over time thanks to a series of conquests, alliances and discoveries. Charles V (1500-1558) built an "empire on which the sun never sets", stretching from Peru to the Philippines, and also including southern Italy and the Netherlands. The country's wealth was due in large part to its colonies: they provided new products, such as sweetcorn, potatoes and green beans, which brought more variety to the European market, while the abundant reserves of gold and other precious metals in the Americas allowed Spain to mint large amounts of currency. Trade between the empire's different territories gave rise to an early form of globalisation.

In the final years of his reign, between 1555 and 1558, Charles V divided his empire in two: he abdicated as Holy Roman Emperor in favour of his brother Ferdinand I (1503-1564), and left the vast majority of his territories to his son Philip II (1527-1598), who in turn passed them down to his own son, Philip III (1578-1621). Philip II and Philip III, who ruled Spain at the time Cervantes was writing, drew their authority from the national army, which was one of the most effective military forces of its time and waged constant campaigns, and from a complex administrative system (given the size of the territory they governed, the task of enforcing royal decrees was delegated to viceroys in each region, who in turn had their own functionaries). However, their military victories, for example at the Battle of Lepanto (1571), which put an end to the Ottoman advance in the Mediterranean, were offset by crushing defeats: in 1588, the Spanish Armada, comprising 130 ships that had set sail to conquer England, was defeated.

ECONOMIC AND SOCIAL TURMOIL

At the dawn of the 17th century, the political decline of the Spanish Empire was already underway, and this was exacerbated by a number of emerging economic and social difficulties. In the second half of the 16th century, an imbalance had appeared due to demographic change coupled with reduced productivity, as some of the peasants who had formerly worked the land instead sought to profit from imports from the colonies. The poorest members of society were hit hard by inflation, and when taxes were suddenly raised in an attempt to rebalance the budget, they migrated en masse to the cities, where they hoped to find a higher quality of life.

At the same time, the supply of precious metals from America was beginning to dwindle, while the administrative and military costs of running the empire remained high. Consequently, the Spanish government struggled to repay its debts. Furthermore, Spain's Muslims, who had been forced to convert to Christianity, threatened to rebel, before finally being driven out of the country in 1609. However, their departure further weakened the Spanish economy, and the gulf between the different social classes was constantly widening. Finally, while the poorest Spaniards bore the brunt of the country's economic troubles, the nobility, which had been pushed out of the political decision-making process in favour of educated advisors, became increasingly restive.

THE SPANISH MONARCHS: CHAMPIONS OF THE COUNTER-REFORMATION

The 16th century was also a turbulent time for religion following the Reformation, which was instigated by the German theologian Martin Luther (1483-1546). In 1517, Luther published his *Ninety-five theses*, in which he denounced the excesses of the Roman Catholic Church, particularly the sale of indulgences, and advocated a return to Christianity's true roots. According to Luther, this should be accomplished by a closer reading of the Bible and the right to practice the religion in the vernacular, not just in Latin. Protestantism then emerged as a dissident branch of Christianity and spread rapidly, particularly in northern Europe. The Roman Catholic Church reacted by holding the Council of Trent between 1545 and 1563, which brought together all the Catholic bishops and sought to reaffirm the fundamental principles of Catholicism and consolidate the Church's position. The resulting Counter-Reformation marked a definitive split between Catholicism and Protestantism.

In the face of the perceived threat presented by this new religious movement, Charles V and Philip II positioned themselves as the champions of Catholic orthodoxy and sought to ensure that the values affirmed by the Council of Trent were scrupulously applied. The last Moors (Muslims) in the country were forced to convert, and the religious order of the Jesuits, founded by the Spaniard Ignatius of Loyola (1491-1556), oversaw the training of priests and the education of young people. Above all, the Inquisition, a tribunal which condemned any practices that did not conform to Catholic principles, stamped out religious dissent in all the territories belonging to the Spanish Crown, with the exception of the Netherlands. The inhabitants of this territory, the majority of whom had embraced Protestantism, did not look favourably on Philip II's religious policy. As a result, the nobility and the middle classes joined forces to demand freedom of worship, and in 1581, following violent clashes, the seven northern provinces split from the

Southern Netherlands, which remained under Spanish rule, to form the Dutch Republic.

SPANISH CULTURAL HEGEMONY DURING THE GOLDEN AGE

Somewhat paradoxically, these dispiriting events were accompanied by a period of exceptional cultural development. This high point in the history of Spanish art is often referred to as the Golden Age (*Siglo de Oro*), beginning with the discovery of the New World by Christopher Columbus (1450/1451-1506) in 1492 and ending in the mid-17th century. Outstanding works in Spanish literature included Luis de Góngora's (1561-1627) highly sophisticated sonnets, Lope de Vega's (1562-1635) baroque plays and the works of Francisco de Quevedo (1580-1645). Picaresque novels, which depicted the fantastic adventures of low-born heroes known as *pícaros*, first appeared in the mid-16th century. The first example of this genre is *The Life of Lazarillo de Tormes and of His Fortunes and Adversities*, which was published anonymously in 1554. This type of novel had no official rules, which meant that it was well suited to Cervantes's time, when traditional structures and frames of reference were being abandoned. Furthermore, it made social criticism and philosophical questioning under the cover of fiction possible.

Other art forms also flourished at this time, including outstanding paintings by El Greco (1541-1614) then Diego Velásquez (1599-1660), and music for the greatest religious ceremonies of the time composed by Tomás Luis de Victoria (1548-1611).

DID YOU KNOW?

El Escorial, to the north-west of Madrid, symbolises Spain's cultural hegemony during the Golden Age. The construction of this multi-purpose centre of power was begun on Philip II's orders in 1563 and completed in 1584, under the direction of Juan Bautista de Toledo (1515-1567) and then Juan de Herrera (1530-1597). It comprises a royal palace, a monastery, a basilica, a library, an art gallery and a mausoleum which houses the remains of Charles V and his successors. The complex provides an excellent illustration of the close links between power, art and religion during the reign of Philip II.

BIOGRAPHY

HUMBLE BEGINNINGS

| Portrait of Miguel de Cervantes.

Cervantes was born in 1547, probably on 29 September, in Alcalá de Henares, near Madrid, to a family of relatively modest means. Very little is known about his mother, Leonora de Cortinas Sánchez, while his father, Rodrigo de Cervantes (1509-1585), was a surgeon who claimed to have noble roots but was in reality the son of a doctor from Córdoba. Rodrigo de Cervantes was often in debt and had frequent brushes with the law, and it seems that he took his wife and five children with him as he roamed across Spain.

We know that the family spent time in Valladolid and Córdoba, but apart from that little is known about the early years of Cervantes's life. The earliest reliable piece of information about him is that by 1566 he had become a student of Juan López de Hoyos (1511-1583), a humanist from Madrid, who published the writer's first poems in 1569.

A TURBULENT YOUTH

In 1568, Cervantes was involved in an altercation, the origins of which remain unclear: nobody knows whether it was motivated by romantic jealousy or by some other cause. Whatever the reason for the dispute, a royal order was issued for the arrest of a man named Miguel de Cervantes for having injured Antonio Sigura. Although it is not possible to say with certainty whether or not the man in question was the renowned author, we do know that Cervantes suddenly left Spain for Italy at around this time and worked as a secretary for the future cardinal Giulio Acquaviva (1546-1574) in Rome. However, this quiet period was short-lived: for reasons that remain unclear, Cervantes soon enlisted in the army. It is possible that he was unable to continue working for Acquaviva; alternatively, he could have been trying to prove that he was a true Spaniard, as some people were casting doubt on his heritage because his family had many features that were typical of *conversos* (Jews who had converted to Christianity). After roaming across various regions of Italy, he fought under Juan of Austria (1545-1578), the half-brother of Philip II of Spain. He took part in the Battle of Lepanto in 1571, a naval battle which aimed to halt the Ottoman advance in the Mediterranean, and lost the use of his left hand. In spite of this injury, he continued to take part in campaigns with the Austrian army for the next several years, before setting off for Spain in 1575.

The expansion of the Ottoman Empire

The Ottoman Empire (1299-1923) was one of the major powers of the Middle Ages and the early modern period. It was founded in modern-day Turkey and its capital was Constantinople from 1453 onwards. At its peak, it stretched across the Near East, Middle East and coasts of North Africa, and extended as far as Vienna in Europe. In the 16th century, during the reigns of Suleiman the Magnificent (1494-1566), Selim II (1524-1574) and Murad III (1546-1595), the empire's expansion on land was accompanied by naval advances in the Mediterranean, primarily to the detriment of the wealthy Italian city-states. Ottoman attacks led the Papal States, the Republic of Venice, Spain and a number of other powers to form an alliance to drive back the invader. The decisive battle took place in Lepanto, close to the western coast of Greece, on 7 October 1571: the purportedly invincible Ottoman fleet sustained heavy losses and, after a day of intense fighting, was forced to retreat. The Battle of Lepanto marked the end of Ottoman expansionism in the Mediterranean.

FROM THE PRISONS OF ALGIERS TO EARLY LITERARY SUCCESS

Not long after leaving Naples, Cervantes's boat was attacked by Ottoman ships. Cervantes and his brother were captured and taken to Algiers, where the writer was identified as a notable prisoner who could be held for ransom. By 1577, his mother had raised enough money to secure the release of one of the two men, and Cervantes sacrificed himself so that his brother Rodrigo could be freed. Cervantes was exceptionally imaginative and made four escape attempts, each more inventive than the last. However, these all failed, either because of bad luck or because he was betrayed by one of his fellow prisoners or a contact outside the prison. These experiences had a lasting impact on him and provided inspiration for much of his writing. Finally, in 1580, an expedition led by members of a religious order managed to negotiate the release or purchase of some captives, including Cervantes, who was finally able to return to his family in Madrid.

This marked the beginning of a period of intense literary productivity and success, in particular thanks to his play *The Siege of Numantia* (1585) and his pastoral romance *La Galatea* (1585). In 1584, he married a woman named Catalina de Salazar y Palacios, who was almost 20 years his junior. In the two years that followed, he wrote and arranged the performance of several plays. Most of these are lost to us today, but we still have their titles.

LATER YEARS

In 1587, Cervantes abandoned writing and his young wife for no apparent reason and moved to Andalusia, where he worked as a collector of supplies and then as a tax collector. In 1592, after being accusing of improperly requisitioning wheat from a monastery, he was excommunicated and imprisoned at Castro del Río. He was released, but was arrested a few years later for misappropriation of the taxes he had collected. It is unclear whether or not he was guilty, but in any case he was imprisoned in Seville in 1597. It was probably during this stint in prison that he came up with the idea for the innovative, parodic novel that would later become *Don Quixote*. After several months in captivity, he was released and disappeared until 1604.

The first part of *Don Quixote*, which reinvented the picaresque novel, was published in 1605 and met with immediate success. However, a year later Cervantes was accused of the murder of a nobleman, which had taken place in front of his house, and this marked another turbulent period for the author. He managed to secure the protection of important figures at Court, and his final years were some of his most productive: the *Novelas ejemplares* were published in 1613, followed by the *Journey to Parnassus* in 1614 and the second part of *Don Quixote* in 1615. Two days before his death, he added the finishing touches to *The Trials of Persiles and Sigismunda*. Cervantes's funeral took place in Madrid on 23 April 1616.

EL INGENIOSO
HIDALGO DON QVI-
XOTE DE LA MANCHA.

*Compuesto por Miguel de Ceruantes
Saauedra.*

DIRIGIDO AL DVQVE DE BEIAR,
Marques de Gibraleon, Conde de Benalcaçar, y Baña-
res, Vizconde de la Puebla de Alcozer, Señor de
las villas de Capilla, Curiel, y
Burguillos

Año,   1605.

CON PRIVILEGIO.
EN MADRID Por Iuan de la Cuesta.

Vendese en casa de Francisco de Robles, librero del Rey nro señor

| Cover of the first edition of *Don Quixote*, 1605.

CHARACTERISTICS OF CERVANTES'S WORK

GENRE

In spite of a series of largely respectable attempts, Cervantes never really broke into any other genres besides the novel and the novella. Even so, the first work he published was a collection of four poems, each of which had a connection to a particular event. Cervantes was keenly aware of his limits, and wrote in his *Journey to Parnassus* that had not been blessed with a gift for poetry. In this ironic, self-deprecating work of verse, the author depicts himself: he sends the best Spanish poets to the mythical Mount Parnassus to duel against their less gifted contemporaries. However, even though Cervantes never achieved real success as a poet, the majority of his prose works also feature some lines of verse, although these do not occupy a prominent position in the text.

His plays were no more successful than his

poetry: only *The Siege of Numantia* met with a positive reception from audiences. Indeed, Cervantes was unable to compete with the innovative work of Lope de Vega, the most famous Spanish playwright of the time. Actors distanced themselves from his work, which was deemed old-fashioned, difficult and overly traditional, in spite of some degree of originality thanks to the elements he borrowed from the theatre of Antiquity. Cervantes then resigned himself to not seeing his plays performed; instead, he published some of them in a collection entitled *Eight Comedies and Eight New Interludes, Never Before Performed* (1615).

A PROLIFERATION OF CHARACTERS AND PLOTS

Cervantes's work as a whole is characterised by several features which work together to make his writing original. His prose texts feature a large number of characters and situations, many of which result in embedded narratives or digressive episodes. These secondary plots allow Cervantes to explore a range of themes, secondary characters and contemporary issues: for example, in *La*

Galatea, Tirsi and Damón frequently interrupt the main plot to discuss romantic passion, one of the novel's central themes.

Besides these interruptions to the main narrative thread, the originality of Cervantes's novels is further accentuated by the fact that they are comprised of distinct episodes that could almost be read independently of one another. Each episode is preceded by a title which indicates the main events that take place in it, and these more or less stand-alone passages follow on from one another to form the complete work.

PARODY AND LITERARY DISCUSSION

The themes of Cervantes's novels, such as love, madness and the supernatural, are nothing new. What makes his work original is his treatment of these themes: his parodic, humorous, innovative approach serves to challenge the literary practices of his time and of previous centuries. For example, *La Galatea* takes the form of a pastoral novel (a love story between two young shepherds with an idyllic setting) in order to contemplate the reasons for this passion, whereas traditional pastoral novels were content to simply describe it. In *The Trials of Persiles and Sigismunda*, Cervantes modernises the Byzantine novel, a sort of adventure story dating from Antiquity. But the clearest example of Cervantes's originality is undoubtedly *Don Quixote*, which parodies the chivalric romances which were popular in the late Middle Ages and depict brave, virtuous knights.

This is not the only example of Cervantes's originality: in the preface to *Don Quixote*, he distances himself from his own text by claiming that the first chapters come from the archives of La Mancha and that the rest of the text is a translation of an Arabic work by an author called Cide Hamete Benengeli. This strategy was widely used at the time, and its effects were twofold: first of all, it allowed Cervantes to protect himself against criticisms of the literary form of his work, and secondly, it meant that he could not be held entirely responsible for its harsh criticism of contemporary Spanish society. Even more surprisingly, in the second part of the novel, Don Quixote and Sancho Panza are aware that they are the heroes of a book and comment on the fact that their adventures have been written down. The lines between reality and fiction have become blurred, and the interplay between the identities of the author, the translator and the characters is strengthened.

NOTABLE WORKS

DON QUIXOTE

Don Quixote comprises two parts, with the second published ten years after the first. The first volume appeared in 1605 and was so popular that pirated versions circulated in secret. This popularity explains why some other authors made ill-advised attempts to profit from the phenomenon: the appearance of a book purporting to be the second part of the novel and signed with the pseudonym Alonso Fernández de Avellaneda in 1614 spurred Cervantes to finish his second volume more quickly. This new book appeared in 1615, and its preface condemns the opportunistic Avellaneda.

Don Quixote tells the story of the outlandish adventures of a minor nobleman, Alonso Quixano, who is so obsessed with chivalric romances that he proclaims himself a knight errant, takes an old horse to be his noble steed, chooses a noble lady love who is really a peasant woman from a neighbouring village and names her Dulcinea del Toboso, and takes on a pragmatic squire, Sancho Panza, whom he meets in the course of his wanderings. Over the course of three successive expeditions (two in the first book and one in the second book), he fights windmills after mistaking them for giants, thinks that a humble inn is a castle, and claims the famous helmet of Mambrino, which is in reality a barber's basin, before returning home, recovering his sanity and dying.

| *Don Quixote and the Windmill* (1863), engraving by Gustave Doré, private collection. Gustave Doré produced 370 illustrations for a French reedition of *Don Quixote* in 1863.

Don Quixote draws on the picaresque novel and was probably influenced by *The Life of Lazarillo de Tormes and of His Fortunes and Adversities.* However, Cervantes's main source of inspiration was the chivalric romances, which he planned to parody. At the time, chivalric romances were a popular literary form with a single main plot and an abundance of fine feelings and noble values. However, the world they depicted bore no resemblance to Spanish society during the reigns of Philip II and Philip III, and Cervantes produced a burlesque narrative by creating a hero who has read these texts and tries to model his life on them. Don Quixote's worldview is based on a literary ideal that he struggles to apply to reality. He blames any failures or setbacks on enchanters that only he is aware of, and is so convinced of the rightness of his cause that he sees trivial gestures as noble and the customs of high society as vulgar. As the story progresses, the reader cannot help but join the author in laughing at this outlandish character who lives in a sort of parallel universe that has come straight from his imagination. The novel's humour is primarily based on the contrast between the absurd situations depicted and the main character's implacable but ridiculous logic.

Don Quixote's squire Sancho Panza serves as a foil to his master: he is unprepared, clumsy, quick to complain and very down-to-earth. Thanks to this character, we witness two languages, two personalities and two ways of seeing the world. Sancho Panza is a sympathetic and colourful character, and adds to the novel's humour: while comedy is present throughout the novel, it is not fully expressed until we see the contrast between Don Quixote and his faithful companion, who provides "a laughter that ridicules but also understands our folly and our humanity" (Martín 1991: 77).

| *Don Quixote and Sancho Panza* (1863), engraving by Gustave Doré, Kharbine-Tapabor collection.

However, *Don Quixote* is more than just a parody of the chivalric romances. The main character's madness means that no criticism or satire of existing institutions is off limits: for example, Philip II's government and Spain under his rule are not spared, especially when Cervantes describes the living conditions of the poorest members of society. Don Quixote criticises all the beliefs, traditions and hierarchies of the Spain of his time at one point or another, but the question of whether his comments are simply a sign of his madness or a veiled expression of Cervantes's ideas remains unanswered. Indeed, perhaps the apparent madman is right and the rest of us prove ourselves foolish by refusing to believe him.

As the hero meets new characters, the fields of action and reflection both expand. While Cervantes's contemporaries had the frame of reference needed to understand the text and the intentions behind it, each subsequent generation has interpreted it differently. Indeed, the fact that the novel deals with universal themes such as madness, illusion, the representation of reality and the impossibility of applying our values to real life means that it will inevitably provoke thought, independent of its original context.

<u>DON QUIXOTE'S INFLUENCE</u>

Cervantes's novel has fascinated generations of writers – for example, the English writer Graham Greene (1904-1991) wrote *Monsignor Quixote*, a pastiche of the work, in 1982, and a number of comics based on the book have been produced – as well as illustrators and painters including Honoré Daumier (1808-1879), Gustave Doré (1832-1883), Pablo Picasso (1881-1973) and Salvador Dalí (1904-1989). It has also been adapted for the theatre, opera and cinema. In 1903, Ferdinand Zecca (1864-1947) and Lucien Nonguet (born in 1868, date of death unknown) adapted *Don Quixote* into a 16-minute silent film. Since then, around 20 films and television series inspired by the knight have been produced. These include the 1992 film begun by Orson Welles (1915-1985), who had long harboured the dream of bringing *Don Quixote* to the screen but remained dissatisfied with the scenes he shot, starting in 1955. The film was completed after Welles's death by his assistant Jesús Franco (1930-2013) and combines classic scenes with a modern reading of the novel. When Terry Gilliam (born in 1940) tried to shoot his take on the novel, *The Man Who Killed Don Quixote*, starring Jean Rochefort, Johnny Depp and Vanessa Paradis, in 2000, he faced a number of problems beyond his control: theft of material, organisational difficulties, Rochefort's illness and torrential downpours meant that the project was eventually shelved. The 2002 documentary *Lost in La Mancha* tells the story of the problems that occurred during filming.

NOVELAS EJEMPLARES

The *Novelas ejemplares* ("Exemplary Novellas"), a collection of 12 texts, appeared in 1613, between the publication of the two parts of *Don Quixote*. However, Cervantes began writing some of these novellas as early as 1590, and two of them were ready for publication by 1605. Writing the book was therefore a lengthy process and occurred as the author roamed from place to place.

Although the 12 novellas share some common features, there is no single unifying theme. They deal with well-established subjects and motifs: impossible marriages, love triangles, chance meetings, secrets and revelations. For example, *La fuerza de la sangre* ("The Strength of Blood") examines the consequences of a womaniser's desires, *El amante liberal* ("The Generous Lover") is about a marriage that is prevented by a fight and a kidnapping, and *El coloquio de los perros* ("The Conversation of the Dogs") takes the form of a critical dialogue between two dogs and their masters.

These brief anecdotes each depict an aspect of the daily life of the time, and their originality and strength lie in their concision and narrative concentration. Digressions, lengthy descriptions and any other superfluous elements have been eliminated, leaving a single straightforward and effective plot. Furthermore, each story features only a small number of characters with little psychological depth, whose reactions shape the course of events. Everything happens in a logical, coherent fashion. Finally, while some of the novellas can be described as realist, meaning that they depict reality in a believable way, others are clearly influenced by the idealistic narratives that also inspired Cervantes when he wrote *La Galatea.*

When Cervantes decided to start writing novellas, he was aware that he was a pioneer in this genre in Spanish, as his were the first original works to be published in the language. However, there were translations of foreign works, notably the *Decameron* by the Italian writer Bocaccio (1313-1375), which had a major influence on European literature from the Renaissance to the 17th century. Furthermore, Cervantes emphasised the distinction between his work and tales, of which there were many in Spanish, by claiming that novellas should focus on a precise moment of crisis, while tales are more diffuse and less tightly structured. This is where the title of the collection comes from: his novellas are exemplary because, in addition to their moral and didactic dimension, they also provide a model of the genre for future writers.

THE TRIALS OF PERSILES AND SIGISMUNDA

The Trials of Persiles and Sigismunda is Cervantes's last book. He probably began it when he returned to Madrid in 1605, and completed it two days before his death in 1616. The writing process was almost certainly not continuous: there must have been breaks, given that Cervantes was also working on the second part of *Don Quixote* and some of the *Novelas ejemplares* at the same time.

The novel tells the story of the two eponymous protagonists, a prince and princess who are both from northern Europe. They are in love and are trying to get to Rome in order to secure the Pope's blessing for their relationship. They adopt the fake names of Periander and Auristela, travel across Europe and weather the dangers presented by a number of secondary characters. The vagaries of the climate and a series of chance encounters mean that they are separated and reunited on multiple occasions before they finally reach their goal. In Rome, their marriage is authorised in a scene that blends elements of fantasy and Christian morality.

In this final work, Cervantes draws on a literary genre from late Antiquity, namely the Byzantine novel, of which *Aethiopica* by the novelist Heliodorus of Emesa (3rd-4th century AD) is an important example. The main subject of this kind of novel is an impossible love between two young people who are depicted in a highly idealised way. In spite of the many obstacles standing in their way, their adventures always have a happy ending. Another feature of the genre is the inclusion of less important secondary narratives alongside the main plot. For example, Cervantes's story is very simple in itself, but is made more complex by several secondary plots: many of the people the protagonists meet tell their own stories, sometimes at considerable length, and this further illuminates the two heroes' love. This kind of digression is an accepted feature of the Byzantine novel, and is also typical of Cervantes's writing, as he had already used it in *Don Quixote*.

Cervantes was not the first author to reinterpret works from Antiquity. The Renaissance humanists, who were the first to rediscover ancient Greek and Roman texts, had already tried writing their own works in this genre, and an earlier Byzantine novel had already been published in Spain in 1552 (*Historia de los amores de Clareo y Florisea, y los trabajos de la sin ventura Isea*, meaning "The History of the Love of Clareo and Florisea, and the Trials of the Unfortunate Isea", by Alonso de Núñez de Reinoso). However,

Cervantes aimed to surpass the work of Heliodorus by incorporating modern, Christian content into his novel. While it is true that there is a significant moral dimension to his work, as was the case for some of his contemporaries, including Jerónimo de Contreras (1505-1582) with *Selva de aventuras* ("Forest of Adventures", 1565) and Lope de Vega with *El peregrino en su patria* ("The Pilgrim in his Own Country", 1604), Cervantes's worldview was less black and white than that of these other authors. In his novel, the lines between good and evil and true and false are less clear, the treatment of faith and philosophy is more nuanced, and as a result the analysis is richer. *The Trials of Persiles and Sigismunda* was Cervantes's favourite of his works and the book he considered the most accomplished. However, although it met with some success in the 17th century, it is far less widely read nowadays.

CERVANTES'S LEGACY

In the centuries following his death, Cervantes has remained a constant source of literary inspiration. Although *Don Quixote* is by far the most widely read and best known, and consequently most influential, of his works, his other books have also had an impact on many writers. For example, *L'Astrée* (1607) by the French author Honoré d'Urfé (1569-1625) probably owes a great deal to the bucolic setting of *La Galatea*.

The basic premise of *Don Quixote* gives the novel a connection to a well-established genre, but thanks to Cervantes's originality the book became a model for later generations. The proliferation of secondary plots and ridiculous characters influenced the burlesque narratives of the 17th century, such as the *Roman comique* (1651 and 1657) by Paul Scarron (1610-1660) and *Le roman bourgeois* (1666) by Antoine Furetière (1619-1688). Furthermore, by introducing characters who are aware that they are fictional, Cervantes was the forerunner of several 18th-century authors, such as Denis Diderot (1713-1784) with *Jacques the Fatalist and His Master* (1778-1780) and Laurence Sterne (1713-1768) with *The Life and Opinions of Tristram Shandy, Gentleman* (1759-1763). In the 20th century, the ambiguous identities of the narrator, writer and hero inspired one of the short stories in Jorge Luis Borges's (1899-1986) collection *Fictions* (1944). In "Pierre Menard, Author of the *Quixote*", the eponymous author undertakes to rewrite *Don Quixote* identically to the original, but justifies each of his narrative choices with a modern argument.

Alongside the authors who were directly inspired by *Don Quixote*, many others have spoken of their profound admiration for the book, including Gustave Flaubert (1821-1880), who wrote of its apparent lack of artifice and constant fusion of illusion and reality, which he saw as deeply poetic, Henry de Montherlant (1895-1972) and Vladimir Nabokov (1899-1977). In 1905, the Spanish author Miguel de Unamuno (1864-1936) wrote a book entitled *Vida de Don Quijote y Sancho* (literally "The Life of Don Quixote and Sancho" but often translated into English as "Our Lord Don Quixote"), a chapter-by-chapter analysis of

Cervantes's novel. Unamuno writes in defence of the main character's madness, comparing it favourably with ordinary people's ostensible common sense and in this way positioning Don Quixote as a sort of philosophical model.

More generally, the blend of fantasy and reality inspired many works of literature in the 20th and 21st centuries. The appearance of inexplicable elements in a rational universe, as happens in both *Don Quixote* and *The Trials of Persiles and Sigismunda*, is known as "magical realism" and represents a significant literary movement, led by influential authors including Italo Calvino (1923-1985), Gabriel García Márquez (1927-2014), Salman Rushdie (born in 1947) and Haruki Murakami (born in 1949). These authors all use their writing to reveal the fantastic elements that are concealed beneath the banality of everyday life.

SUMMARY

- Miguel de Cervantes was one of the major authors of the Spanish Golden Age, a period of significant cultural development which began in the late 15th century and ended in the mid-17th century. At the same time, Spain entered a phase of political decline at the start of the 17th century and the difficulties of running the Spanish Empire meant that living conditions deteriorated for much of the population.
- Cervantes's life was particularly turbulent: he spent time as the secretary of a future cardinal, a soldier during the Battle of Lepanto, a prisoner of war, a tax collector and even a fugitive accused of murder.
- He only began to focus more closely on literature from 1580 onwards. His first success as a writer came in 1585, with the pastoral novel *La Galatea* and the play *The Siege of Numantia*. However, his literary activity was interrupted by a period of exile in Andalusia and some brushes with the law.
- He was at his most productive in the final

years of his life, as three of his major works were published between 1605 and his death in 1616: *Don Quixote*, the *Novelas ejemplares* and *The Trials of Persiles and Sigismunda*, which he considered to be his most accomplished work.

- Cervantes tended to work within existing genres, such as the picaresque novel and the Byzantine novel, and deal with traditional themes (love, madness, and so on), but was undeniably original in the way he transformed them by parodying them or adapting them for Spanish culture in books that were characterised by humour and social criticism.
- His works, and in particular *Don Quixote*, influenced many later authors, who drew heavily on his humour, his narrative techniques and his reflections on reality and illusion.

We want to hear from you!
Leave a comment on your online library
and share your favourite books on social media!

FURTHER READING

BIBLIOGRAPHY

- Becker, D. (2002) *Cervantès, l'homme des masques et des secrets*. [Online]. [Accessed 26 October 2017]. Available from: <http://www.clio.fr/bibliotheque/cervantes_l_homme_des_masques_et_des_secrets.asp>

- Canavaggio, J. (No date) Cervantès, Miguel de (1547-1616). *Encyclopaedia Universalis*. [Online]. [Accessed 10 March 2015]. Available from: <http://www.universalis-edu.com/encyclopedie/miguel-decervantes/>

- De Cervantes, M. (2014) *The Trials of Persiles and Sigismunda*. Overland Park, Kansas: Digireads.

- De Cervantes, M. (2008) *Exemplary Stories*. Trans. Lipson, L. Oxford: Oxford University Press.

- De Cervantes, M. (2003) *Don Quixote*. Trans. Rutherford, J. London: Penguin.

- Joset, J. (1995) Cervantès (1547-1616). *Patrimoine littéraire européen. Établissement des genres et retour du tragique*. Brussels: De Boeck Université. pp. 883-885.

- Lapeyre, H. (No date) Espagne (Le territoire et les hommes) – De l'unité politique à la guerre civile.

Encyclopaedia Universalis. [Online]. [Accessed 17 February 2017]. Available from: <http://www.universalis-edu.com/encyclopedie/espagne-le-territoire-et-les-hommes-de-l-unite-politique-a-la-guerre-civile/>

- Larousse.fr (No date) *Arts du Siècle d'or espagnol*. [Online]. [Accessed 26 October 2017]. Available from: <http://www.larousse.fr/encyclopedie/divers/arts_du_Si%C3%A8cle_dor_espagnol/181572>

- Larousse.fr (No date) *Cervantès*. [Online]. [Accessed 26 October 2017]. Available from: <http://www.larousse.fr/encyclopedie/personnage/Miguel_de_Cervant%C3%A8s/112410>

- (2010) Les grands héros de la littérature : Don Quichotte. *Le Magazine littéraire*, 1.

- Martín, A. L. (1991) *Cervantes and the Burlesque Sonnet*. Berkeley, Los Angeles and Oxford: University of California Press.

- Molho, M. (No date) Picaresque, roman. *Encyclopaedia Universalis*. [Online]. [Accessed 17 February 2017]. Available from: <http://www.universalis-edu.com/encyclopedie/romanpicaresque/>

- Riley, E. C. and Cruz, A. J. (No date) Miguel de Cervantes. *Encyclopaedia Britannica*. [Online]. [Accessed 26 October 2017]. Available from: <https://www.britannica.com/biography/Miguel-de-Cervantes>

- Sesé, B. (No date) Don Quichotte, livre de M. de Cervantès. *Encyclopaedia Universalis*. [Online]. [Accessed 10 March 2015]. Available from: <http://www.universalis-edu.com/encyclopedie/don-quichottelivre-de-m-de-cervantes/>

ADDITIONAL SOURCES

- Canavaggio, J. (1990) *Cervantes*. Trans. Jones, J. R. New York: W. W. Norton & Company, Inc.

- Cascardi, A. J. ed. (2008) *The Cambridge Companion to Cervantes*. Cambridge: Cambridge University Press.

- Cerf, N. (2016) *Don Quixote by Miguel de Cervante (Book Analysis)*. Trans. de Dorlodot, S. Brussels: Plurilingua Publishing.

- González Echevarría, R. (2005) *Cervantes'Don Quixote: A Casebook*. New York: Oxford University Press.

- McCrory, D. P. (2006) *No Ordinary Man: The Life and Times of Miguel de Cervantes*. Mineola, New York: Dover Publications, Inc.

ICONOGRAPHIC SOURCES

- Monument in memory of Miguel de Cervantes, Plaza de España, Madrid. Royalty-free reproduction picture.

- Portrait of Miguel de Cervantes. Royalty-free reproduction picture.

- Cover of the first edition of *Don Quixote*, 1605. Royalty-free reproduction picture.

- *Don Quixote and the Windmill* (1863), engraving by Gustave Doré, private collection. Royalty-free reproduction picture.

- *Don Quixote and Sancho Panza* (1863), engraving by Gustave Doré, Kharbine-Tapabor. Royalty-free reproduction picture.

IMPROVE YOUR GENERAL KNOWLEDGE

IN A BLINK OF AN EYE !

www.50minutes.com

Although the editor makes every effort to verify the accuracy of the information published, 50Minutes. com accepts no responsibility for the content of this book.

© 50MINUTES.com, 2017. All rights reserved.

www.50minutes.com

Ebook EAN: 9782808005203

Paperback EAN: 9782808005210

Legal Deposit: D/2017/12603/798

Cover image: © *Miguel de Cervantes*, Eduardo Balaca

Digital conception by Primento, the digital partner of publishers.